Deepak Bajaj is an ace motivation [...] life and business transformation co [...] author of 3 books in 8 languages.

A master of personal transformation, Deepak has been on a mission to inspire and empower people to be the best they can be for the last 2 decades. Millions of people from 150-plus countries have been achieving their dreams faster with his books, live events, online courses, and video training. His videos have already received more than 160 million views on social media.

All three of Deepak's books *Be a Network Marketing Millionaire, Achieve More, Succeed Faster* and *Be a Social Media Millionaire* have been established as the most read and recommended books in the direct selling industry.

Deepak's live events and online courses have been globally recognized for their incredible results, and more than 1.7 million people have already attended his training sessions. He has been featured in various magazines and has received various awards, including Best Direct Selling Trainer 2020& 2022, Best Debut Author 2018, Best Entrepreneurship Trainer & Coach, etc. He has been a Josh Talks speaker 3 times and a TEDx speaker as well.

He is a regular speaker at annual conventions, leadership programs, conferences, corporate events, etc. and has contributed to the transformation of so many individuals, start ups, and corporates with his life and business transformation coaching.

Connect with him on all major social media platforms and at www.deepakbajaj.biz.

Other books by Deepak Bajaj:

- Be a Network Marketing Millionaire
- Achieve More, Succeed Faster
- Be a Social Media Millionaire

Network Marketing in

60
Minutes

DEEPAK BAJAJ

MANJUL

Manjul Publishing House

First published in India by

MANJUL

Manjul Publishing House

• C-16, Sector 3, Noida, Uttar Pradesh 201301, India
Website: www.manjulindia.com

Registered Office:
• 10, Nishat Colony, Bhopal 462 003 – India

Distribution Centres:
Ahmedabad, Bengaluru, Bhopal, Kolkata, Chennai,
Hyderabad, Mumbai, New Delhi, Pune

This edition first published in 2022
Second impression 2023

ISBN 978-93-5543-153-0

Cover design: Bhavi Mehta

Feedback for Deepak's Books and Training

Deepak Bajaj is India's leading direct selling expert. His work is showing people the way to change their life.

—Sh. Som Parkash, Union Minister for Commerce and Industry, Govt. of India

Deepak Bajaj is among the top 5 biggest contributors to the Indian direct selling industry.

—Centre of Excellence for Direct Selling in Academics, Shoolini University & IDSA

Deepak Bajaj has started a new revolution in the training and education methods of the Indian direct selling industry. He has been working continuously for the upliftment of direct sellers with his books, training programs, online courses, and free videos.

—Direct Selling Today Magazine

I am very happy to see the making of Mr. Deepak Bajaj. Whatever he has learned in his direct selling journey, he is teaching to others through his training and helping them succeed faster.

—Dr. Surekha Bhargava, veteran direct seller

Deepak Bajaj's books are full of ideas, skills, tools, and solutions that can enlighten, inspire, and empower everyone to build a dream life.

—Hindustan Times

Deepak Bajaj's events are a perfect place to get the right vision, professional guidance, and best learnings from the experts of the field. Deepak Bajaj's training is contributing to the massive growth of the Indian direct selling industry.

—Nilesh Patrawala, veteran direct seller

Every direct seller and those who target to become a millionaire should read this book.

—Kailash Bhattad, CEO, Mi Lifestyle Marketing
Global Private Limited

Deepak Bajaj is India's #1 authority on network marketing, an entrepreneurship consultant, a life coach, a transformational trainer, and an inspirational speaker all rolled into one.

—Invincible Magazine

The energy, learnings, practical tools, and transformation that I have found in Deepak Bajaj's event is something I have never seen before.

—Dr. Surender Vats, veteran direct seller

Deepak Bajaj is working day and night for the development of the right tools, training, and the complete ecosystem for the success of direct sellers and the direct selling industry.

—UP Plus Newspaper

Deepak Bajaj has helped me with strategies and processes for my business. He has taken my career graph from 0 to 100. He is a great coach.

—Payal Kothari, Gut Health Coach,
Founder of INUEN & Gut Avatar

Everything in Deepak Bajaj's training events feels like a dream come true. Deepak Bajaj's training has everything you need to succeed in direct selling. This industry needs more people like Deepak to grow not only in India but in the world, too.

—*Dipal Patrawala, veteran direct seller*

One of the best books on how to achieve big in network marketing. It's a perfect gift for the teammates to make them serious in business.

—*Mubeen Muhammad, Veteran Direct Seller*

Deepak's books are like the Geeta or the Quran of network marketing.

—*Dr. Akhtar Khanwala, veteran direct seller*

Deepak Sir's courses are a million-dollar jackpot at a throwaway price. These are the best programs anyone can get.

—*Suveer Singh*

The best part about Deepak Bajaj's training is duplication. My entire team is able to follow his concepts easily.

—*Rashmi Saxena*

All the mindset, skillset, and toolset that you need for building a big business has been covered in one single course by Deepak Bajaj.

—*Shuchi Caire*

What I could not learn in 20 years of my network marketing career, I have got in Deepak Bajaj's online course. It's out of this world.

—*Jay Prakash Maurya*

Deepak Bajaj's courses are not just about building business, but also about how to live life in the right way. It has totally changed every aspect of my life.

—*Kiran John*

This one book is enough for success in direct selling.

—*Mukesh Singh*

I have become unstoppable. I got 10 years ahead with this great book.

—*Lomesh Choudhary*

I have become a totally different person after attending Deepak sir's course. Everyone around me is giving me compliments that I have changed a lot and my business is also growing.

—*Nargis Sultana*

I got answers to all my questions in Deepak Bajaj's books. These have given rocket-like speed to my business.

—*Nitu Jindal*

After doing Deepak sir's course I am feeling such positive vibes in me, which I never felt before. His course is not just for business results but it's a life transformation course that will help you everywhere in life.

—*Viren Jumani*

Deepak Bajaj's books are a one-stop solution for network marketing. Strongly recommended for those who want to avoid mistakes and achieve success faster.

—*Vijay Tetarwal*

Amazing books for beginners, doers, experts, and trainers.

—*Pradeep Choudhery*

Dedication

To each one of you who not only has dreams but also has the drive and commitment to work for those dreams.

More changes have happened in the network marketing industry in the last 2 to 3 years than in the last 2 to 3 decades. This book is a total personal and business transformation tool that will empower you to achieve massive success in this new age of network marketing.

Growing up in a village, studying in local schools, facing financial struggles, moving from having a job to being an entrepreneur, making mistakes, and starting all over again from zero… I have been through all of it, and I know how it feels. Trust me, you have the seeds of greatness within you, and this book is my contribution to bringing out the legend in you.

Now is your time to rise.

Go for your dreams.

Stay unstoppable.

Deepak Bajaj's Direct Selling Journey

The transformation of Deepak Bajaj from a shy village boy to one of the top performers of the direct selling industry and then to a leading life and business transformation coach is a source of inspiration and strength for everyone. Deepak has come a long way and is living proof of what can be achieved with clear vision, absolute faith, the right values, and tireless hard work.

Deepak was born into a family of government employees in a remote village in Haryana, India and studied in different Hindi-medium government schools. His father passed away after a two-year-long battle with cancer when Deepak was 8 years old. Deepak had a tough childhood laden with financial challenges and many other difficulties. But all those years, Deepak grew up with one dream in mind – One day I will be a big man.

Determined to make it big, Deepak cleared the CAT exam and completed his MBA from a leading management institute. He started his corporate career with a sales job at a leading automobile MNC and rose to the rank of regional manager in record time.

On 28th June 2007, he started a network marketing business part-time alongside his job and worked aggressively with a game plan, which is now famous across the world as the 90-day game plan. He worked non-stop, day and night for the next 3 months on a grueling schedule, set new records at his network marketing company, and resigned from his corporate job after the 3 months.

Deepak was excellent at sales, but he had no experience with direct selling. He did not have any training programs or support system, his teammates could not duplicate his working style, and his business crashed to zero, putting his family through their worst financial crisis ever. It was a tough phase, and all his relatives and friends suggested he go back to his job. Any ordinary person would have quit in that situation, and even Deepak felt like quitting sometimes. But instead, he worked harder, learned more, and continued moving forward with the philosophy that what doesn't break you, makes you stronger.

He became a student of the business and started learning the best practices for success from across the globe. He read hundreds of books, did every online course possible, and traveled around the world to receive the best training from the leaders in the field. The more rejections he faced, the more time and money he invested into his training and development. Gradually, he started creating his own unique programs and systems which were never heard of before in the industry, and he set record after record in the business.

As he started expanding his business in multiple locations, he faced many challenges along the way and many of his teams crashed, but Deepak used every failure to improve his systems. He created several duplicable tools that anyone could use to grow their business anywhere, irrespective of their age, background, location, education, gender, or financial situation. Those system and tools turned his business into a passive income-generating machine from January 2009 onwards.

Millions of people at different network marketing companies have already fulfilled their dreams and achieved good ranks in their companies using his tools and systems. His three books *Be a Network Marketing Millionaire, Achieve More, Succeed Faster* and *Be a Social Media Millionaire* have already become the most read and recommended books in the entire direct selling industry. His books have been translated into 8 languages, and direct sellers in every company are advised to read these books to succeed in this business. These books are full of strategies, tools, techniques, and insights that can help anyone achieve massive success in the business as well as in life.

With almost two decades of incredible experience, Deepak has become a brand unto himself and is considered a living legend in the direct selling industry. He has received the Best Direct Selling Trainer & Coach award multiple times. He has been featured in various magazines and has received various awards including Best Debut Author 2018, Best Entrepreneurship Trainer & Coach, etc. He has been a Josh Talks and TEDx speaker multiple times. Recently, he was recognized to be among the top 5 biggest contributors to the Indian direct selling industry by the Centre of Excellence for Direct Selling in Academics, Shoolini University & IDSA.

Since 10th June 2018, he has been working aggressively toward the growth of direct selling industry by training and coaching direct sellers and direct selling companies across the globe. Millions of people from 150+ countries are actively following his work on social media. He is an international master NLP practitioner and has received training from the world's best trainers and leaders in USA, Singapore, Europe, Bangkok, and India.

Deepak's live stadium events are always packed with a

full house because of their powerful international content, unique NLP-based methodology, activity-based interactive learning style, and real life tools and techniques that give instant results and lasting transformation to the participants. More than 1.7 million people have already attended his training sessions.

He is a regular keynote speaker at various events, distributor meets, seminars, annual conventions, leadership training programs, etc. and is looked upon as the lighthouse of the direct selling industry. He is also a consultant for companies and helps them multiply their sales, performance, culture, and systems. Direct sellers from network marketing companies across the world consider Deepak's online courses to be the most affordable, trusted, and fastest way to achieve results.

Deepak is an avid reader, a world traveler, and an adventure sports enthusiast.

Deepak's life mission is to empower people to be the best they can be. Deepak and his team have been constantly working on creating tools, online courses, and training events that can help people achieve their goals faster and be happier.

You can connect with Deepak on various social media platforms and at www.deepakbajaj.biz.

How to get the most out of this book

This book is my dream project. Within it, I have condensed my two decades of experience working with and training over 1.7 million people in the form of 60 chapters that anyone can read in 60 minutes. Here are a few special features of this book:

- This book contains 60 of the most important insights about the network marketing business that will serve as guiding principles and working strategies for you.

- Each chapter has one key strategy written in a large font on one page so that you can grab it just by looking at it. A detailed explanation of every insight is given on the adjacent page.

- All chapters are independent of each other. You can open any page of this book and start reading from anywhere.

- Sharing and teaching are the best ways to remember what you read. I recommend that once you read any chapter, you share it with as many people as you can via phone calls, Zoom meetings, events, WhatsApp, Instagram, Facebook, Telegram, or any other platform. The more you share it, the better you'll remember it. Also, I believe it's everyone's duty to share good things with their fellow human beings.

- Please read all 60 chapters; you never know which idea could be the turning point of your business and life.

- Don't forget to share your feedback with me.
  Go all out and live your dreams.
  Your transformation begins today.
  Keep growing.

—Deepak Bajaj

1

If you have started taking action
toward achieving your dreams,
you are already a winner;
the biggest losers are those
who have not yet started.

A beginning has incredible power. It's the first step toward a totally new life. The fact that you have chosen to start a network marketing business is proof that you want to make the rest of your life the best of your life. You are not among the millions who just sit around complaining and blaming others. You are already a winner, my friend, and I am extremely proud of you.

Now, as you move forward, always remember these four things:

- One small action is better than a thousand noble intentions. A decision means nothing if you don't take action on it. So boldly take action.

- People will laugh at you, ridicule you, criticize you, and try to pull you down, but you must not stop because of other people's opinions and judgments.

- Don't stop midway. There will be times when doubts creep in, when you feel tired, or when the results do not turn out as you had expected. You may feel like quitting during those dark hours, but just remember why you started and carry on. Don't stop when you are tired; stop only after achieving what you were going for.

- Your darkest days will teach you the brightest lessons.

2

You can come into this business by chance, but you cannot become a millionaire by chance.

I don't know what made you venture into this business, but since you have and since you are reading this book, I want you to remember that success in network marketing demands all the qualities and virtues that are required for success in any other job, profession, or business.

If somebody told you that network marketing is a zero-investment business, they were lying to you. You don't have to invest any money in this business, but to get the results you expect, you need to work hard every day and have faith, confidence, and a professional work ethic. One of the biggest mistakes people make in this business is to judge it based on what they have invested to get their business off the ground. You should evaluate it on the basis of what the business can give you – the returns are potentially infinite.

If you are really committed to succeeding, be willing to learn and work as per the operating system of this business.

You get your business ID free with product shopping, but you need to earn success, respect, and a reputation with consistent hard work.

3

People don't quit this business after hearing a 'no' from some of their prospects. People quit because their list is too small.

After working with 1.7 million people over 15 years, I have realized that the biggest reason why people quit this business is not that a few of their prospects said 'no' to them. It's because their prospect list is too small.

Imagine you went up to 6 people and shared your business opportunity, and all 6 said no. If your list consisted only of those 6 people, your business would have ended right there. But if your list had 300 names, you would not have even begun. You'd just be warming up. 98% of your prospects would still be left.

When you focus on constantly adding new names to your list and train your associates to also expand their lists, you will always have a big, thriving business and you will be able to retain more people.

While most network marketers keep complaining that their list is exhausted, there is another category of distributors who have a big list, good influence, and good presentation skills, but are too shy to approach people. I want to remind such network marketers that looking at your list will not make you rich; only converting your list into quality meetings will move your business forward.

4

Nothing is easy or difficult in itself;
you make it easy or difficult through
your attitude and actions.

My wife makes excellent chapatis, but I can't. I can train 10,000 people in one single event, but my wife finds it difficult to address even 10 people for 5 minutes. My son plays basketball the whole day during hot summer days, but I can't do it for even 30 minutes. There are people who can fly an airplane or a spaceship and countless others who are afraid of riding a motorcycle.

Ask yourself: are things difficult, or are you just making them so? Please remember that anything can be easy if you are willing to learn it and constantly practice it till you become a master at it.

Don't abandon a life-changing opportunity just because you have never done it before or it looks difficult. If any of the activities in this business look difficult to you right now, remember that walking, writing, driving, and many other things that you can easily do today also seemed difficult to you at some point. Regular practice made them easier to do. Every hero started from zero. Today is your turn. Learn something new right now.

5

If I don't feel good about the business, why should I venture into it? But if it is actually good, then why should I hesitate to share it with others?

Some people ask me how I earned two lakh rupees in income in the first month of my direct selling business while working part-time at my job in 2007.

One of the key reasons why I achieved huge success is that I shared my business opportunity with a lot of people everyday with 100% faith. If you read it carefully, you will find two magic ingredients hidden in the above statement:

- I had 100% faith in my business.
- I shared my business plan with the maximum number of people every day.

You cannot expect to be successful if you miss either of them. Selling skills are definitely important, but what is more important is your absolute faith in whatever you are selling. In my last two decades of sales experience, I have realized selling is nothing but a transfer of emotions. During all your meetings, you pass onto your prospect whatever you have inside you. If you have faith, you will transfer faith; if you have doubt, you will transfer doubt. Faith also multiplies your confidence and uplifts your body language.

Remember, you can't fool your teammates and prospects, so either work with full faith or don't do it at all.

6

Ice on your head,
sugar in your mouth, and
shoes on your feet.

We are in a people business, and dealing with people can be difficult at times. Everyone is loaded with their own unique attitude, mindset, and emotions. When you are dealing with people, you are actually dealing with their emotions. The golden rule of *"ice on your head, sugar in your mouth, and shoes on your feet"* can help you manage people better. Always remember:

- Stay calm in every situation. Things will not always go the way you planned and people will not always behave or talk the way you expected. It will hurt, but the magic lies in staying calm and letting the storm pass. Practice keeping your head cool during all situations. Issues are often temporary, but your reaction can cause permanent damage.

- Make it a rule that any words that leave your mouth do not insult or demean anyone. Give truthful feedback wherever required, but don't criticize. Words can make or break relationships. I have lost a few good teams because I broke this rule.

- Although network marketing is a home-based business, you need to step out and actively participate in meetings, events, training sessions, home meetings, celebrations, and casual get-togethers.

7

If Osama Bin Laden could find
thousands of people who were ready
to die for him, why can't you find a
few people who want to live
good lives?

One of the key objectives in network marketing is to get some people on our team who are just as hungry as we are to change their lives. Just think: if thousands of network marketing leaders around the world since the 1940s have found their key associates, why can't you find leaders who will passionately build their fortune with you? You just need to follow the right business-building principles and continue the search till you find them.

Getting good leaders is like finding diamonds in a mine. Sometimes you need to remove tons of stones to get to the real diamonds. The only mistake people make is that they stop digging too early. So hold on to your dreams and continue working.

If you don't know how to find and develop leaders, don't worry. All the top leaders also didn't know how to recruit, train, and empower people when they started. Everyone learned it during their network marketing journey. You will also master it. You can learn the depth-and-width building process from your uplines, through my first book, *Be a Network Marketing Millionaire,* or through my live events and online courses.

8

Your team will not do what you say; your team will do what you consistently do.

Let's be clear about one thing – you cannot fool people. Don't expect your team to aggressively expand to new cities if you have never built a business outside your own city. Don't expect your team to win a foreign trip contest if you won your last foreign trip 5 years ago. Your team will never do personal sponsoring every week if you don't even remember the last time you did it.

Leadership is demonstrating, not preaching. People don't hear from their ears; people hear from their eyes. Please don't become a trainer or preacher for your team. YouTube and the Internet are already full of them. Your team needs a true leader who is a doer. Whatever you want your team to do, you must do it consistently. Remember, the key is not to do good things once in a while, but to do them consistently.

During one of my live events, UCY (Unleash the Champion in You), a participant asked me, "How long should we do it for?" My answer is forever. If something is good and gives you good results, why would you want to stop doing it?

9

Ordinary people with extraordinary focus can accomplish extraordinary achievements.

Most people start network marketing as a side hustle. They start building this business part-time along with some other job, business, or profession. They also have other family and social commitments, so this business doesn't get the time and attention that it requires, and hence it never takes off. Then people quit and start criticizing the business.

The rule is simple – the grass will be greener only where you water it. If you want this business to give you excellent returns, you need to first give it your time and effort. And not just this business – any sport, relationship, job, profession, or serious pursuit will give you results only when you focus on it. As Stephen R. Covey said, the main thing is to keep the main thing the main thing.

Focus is your biggest edge. Even if you don't have adequate talent, education, communication skills, selling skills, personality, or stage performance skills, you can still be a top achiever if you have focus. Stay committed, keep growing, and continue finding people who are more talented and skillful than you. You can definitely build a big business empire. This business always gives excellent results; people just don't take it seriously.

10

God will give you a big team only
when you are ready for it.

Leading a team is a big responsibility. When people start doing business with you, they place their dreams and hopes in your hands. It's your duty to take care of them. You started the business and got the first 10 to 12 people into the business. If you are unable to guide and lead these 10 to 12 people to success, how can God give you any more people?

Everyone wants to join up with and stay with a good leader. So while building your team, please remember that you will not attract who you want, but you will attract who you are. Make a list of all the qualities that a good upline or leader has and then start working to develop those qualities within yourself. Your job is to transform yourself into a great leader.

More changes have happened in the network marketing business in the last 2 to 3 years than in the last 2 to 3 decades. It's all new age network marketing now. People's habits, ways of living, technology, and lifestyles have changed rapidly. You cannot survive and thrive with the same old mindset, skillset, and toolset. Being a captain is different from being a player. Time to change gears and become capable of leading a team.

11

Slow and steady never wins the race;
it's fast and consistent that
wins the race.

I have met thousands of network marketers who feel proud of not quitting this business for many years or decades. I appreciate their spirit and commitment, but just staying in the business is not enough. Consistently working and getting better is absolutely essential to becoming a winner. You have started an awesome business, but the business will work only when you do the work.

The old story of the hare and the tortoise is one of the biggest lies ever told to us. The hero of the story, the tortoise, is grossly slow and wins the race only because his competitor was sleeping. This doesn't happen in the real world. Slow and steady never wins the race; it's fast and consistent that does. You cannot become the first mover of network marketing, but you can definitely become a fast mover, and that is the only way to live your dream life.

I have trained 1.7 million network marketers from 1000s of companies so far and I have not seen any income plan that gives income on the basis of seniority; your income is based solely on rank, volume, and structure. So act bigger and faster to stay ahead.

12

Success in this business is not a
revolution, it's an evolution.

I have seen a lot of network marketers who somehow manage to earn one big achievement, like getting a new car, winning a contest, buying a new property, or becoming a full-timer in the hope that it will create a big and stable business. While some people buy these things using their earnings, there are many others who take loans or use shortcuts or unfair practices to buy these things while under the illusion that these achievements will build their brand.

Please remember all these achievements are necessary and should happen at the right time, but a big and stable business is built on the foundation of the right systems and field practices, not on any one big achievement. When you and your whole team focus on constant learning, systematic working, and event-based business, it will automatically lead to a big ongoing business.

I have been following a rule since childhood which I call the Power of Extra – do whatever is expected from you, and then do a little extra. These little extra improvements will, over time, empower you to evolve into an unstoppable direct selling leader. Take daily steps for long-term stability and not just temporary one-time income.

13

The question is not network marketing any more; the real question is you.

When I started my network marketing business in 2007, our biggest challenge was convincing people about network marketing, but nowadays everyone knows about it and what it offers. Today, prospects don't ask why should they venture into this business; rather, they want to know why should they join up with you.

You are meeting people and telling them that their life can change by entering into business with you. They will naturally want to know if your own life has changed after working for so many months or years. Talking about your company or your upline's achievements can help you for sometime, but ultimately you need to give your prospects a strong reason why should they trust you for fulfilling their dreams.

If your child was not well, would you look for the best doctor, or just any doctor? Would you look for just any teacher or the best teacher possible for your child? We all look for the best doctors, teachers, and lawyers, so the time is near when people will look for the best network marketers to venture into business with. So work properly and earn the reputation of being a successful network marketer.

14

Shift your business from being person-driven to system-driven.

You will meet a lot of people who think network marketing is good but that there is no stability in this business. Look at any business around you and you will realize that stability comes from system and scale. If you want scale, stability, and growth, you need to shift your business from being a person-driven business to a system-driven business.

As per business dictionary.com, a system is a set of detailed methods, procedures, and routines created to carry out a specific activity. In our business, a system is a set of programs, activities, tools, and processes that anyone does on a daily basis to get the best results for the time and effort invested into the business.

A system is especially important as your team starts growing and different people start building businesses in different locations. A system makes success easier and faster for everyone. Success is multiplied manifold when everyone in your team follows the same working style, events, and tools. Give power to your people and empower them with the right system so that the business continues to grow with or without you.

Remember, there is no secret to success; there is always a system to success.

15

You will never get a million friends
without making a few enemies.

One of the biggest reasons why people are not able to build their business, start their YouTube channel, write a book or a post on Instagram, or do anything new is that they are scared of critics. People keep worrying that if they post something, someone may write a negative comment, some people may dislike it, or that others will criticize it.

This is your life, my friend, and you are here to live life on your terms. Other people's happiness and approval is not needed for you to rise and grow. If you do the right things, you will grow in life, and a genuine friend or well-wisher will never criticize your efforts to grow.

Always remember that some people will never like what you do, however good it may be. It's not about you; it's about them. Never worry about pleasing people, especially those who don't really care about you. If you want to please people, please your family or team by achieving something so big that they are proud of you.

Never give up on your goal because of fear of other people's criticism. Once you achieve your goal, the opinions of your critics will automatically change.

16

Manage your business with data and not just emotions.

99 percent of network marketing leaders operate their business solely based on emotions. When do they think of doing a program? When the team demands it or when business seems to be going down. What do they ask while reviewing their teammates? "How is the business going?", or "What you think is going wrong?", etc.

The rule is simple – if you ask vague questions, you get vague answers. If you can focus your reviews and discussions on numbers, most of the time you will get better answers and you will be able to make better decisions. Don't ask how the program was; rather, track how many people attended the event and how much business was generated within one week of the program. You can also track how many new rank achievers were present at the event and how many people stayed at the event till the end, or how many associates were present at post-event meetings.

When you start reviewing the performance of your teammates and your business using numbers, your judgment will be more accurate and your decisions will be smarter. Yes, you should definitely consider your feelings and intuition, but remember, we are in the numbers business, and numbers don't lie.

17

Success is not owned, success is rented, and the rent is due every single day.

When I worked my regular job, there was a rule in our sales department that anybody would get applause and appreciation only once for any achievement. If you wanted applause again, then you'd have to accomplish some new achievement. Also, concepts like Six Sigma, kaizen, and continuous improvement were deeply instilled in us. One key reason why I could earn huge income, respect, and influence in network marketing from the very beginning is that I built my network marketing business with those same values and principles.

The rule is simple, my friend –you are either growing or dying. You cannot achieve something once in this business and expect the world to give you lifelong respect for that same old achievement.

I always say in my leadership workshops that leadership is dynamic. Once you become a leader, your responsibility doesn't decrease, it actually multiplies. Now more eyes are looking at you and you need to constantly give new reasons for your teammates to follow you. Make sure your rank, income, achievements, and lifestyle improve regularly. As your rank and influence grow, never stop doing the core activities and continue improving yourself to do more faster.

18

The question is not whether we
should use social media or not; the
real question is how to use it smartly
to build a big business.

If you are still doubting whether to use social media to expand your business, you are already late. And what do you do when you are late? You speed up. So if you are not getting good business from social media already, you need to immediately speed up your social media game.

Social media and online technologies have already redefined the core activities of network marketing. Social media has proven to be a great help in list expansion, prospecting, team retention, establishing leadership, geographical expansion, etc. When combined with online technologies and the right tools, it can give you huge leverage. Why do I recommend using social media for building business? I believe network marketers should be present wherever there are people, and since people are present on social media, every smart network marketer should also be present on social media.

Social media mastery is such a big subject that it's tough to cover all the details here, but I highly recommend you start using social media as an integral part of your business strategy. If you need complete guidance on how to use social media to build a big business online, refer to my #1 bestselling book, *Be a Social Media Millionaire*.

19

Some people will join you to do business with you, and some will join to introduce you to other people who will.

Sooner or later you have to accept the fact that not everybody who ventures into this business with you will finish with you. People will keep coming and going. The problem starts when you begin expecting that everyone who listens to your presentation should join, that everyone who joins should come to meetings, that everyone who attends meetings should build business seriously, that everyone who is serious should become a full-timer or buy a particular car, etc.

Not everyone can be a doctor or a CA. Not everyone is fit to be in the police or the army. So why do you feel that everybody should do network marketing? Everyone can do this business, but not everyone will. It's purely their choice. You also took your own time.

Give all your care and support to your teammates, but remember that some people will come to do business with you and some will come to introduce you to other people who will. The top leaders in 70% of my legs were not those whom I had personally sponsored. They were introduced into the business by someone who quit, but I continued working with them and built a big business empire with them. Have faith, support everyone, and keep going stronger.

20

There's no such thing as good or bad meetings. Either there are meetings or there are not.

I have seen a countless number of network marketers who keep waiting for their upline to come and share the business plan, because they feel their upline can conduct meetings better. There are many others who keep postponing their meetings because they doubt if they will be able to deliver the perfect presentation.

If you or someone you know falls in this category, please remember these four invaluable insights regarding business meetings:

- This business will become totally yours only after you start conducting your business meetings yourself.

- One meeting by itself doesn't decide whether the prospect will venture into business with you or not. The final result depends a lot on what you do before and after the business presentation. Sales closing is the result of several meetings – some before the business presentation and some after. Never do the business presentation meeting if you cannot conduct a minimum of 3 follow-through meetings in the next month.

- The person who is viewing the presentation is more important than who is delivering it.

- There's no such thing as good or bad meetings. Either there are meetings or not.

21

Success is boring.

There is only one route to achieve massive success in anything – identifying the core activities essential for success in that venture and then getting obsessive about doing those activities consistently, day after day. Success needs mastery, mastery comes from consistency, and consistency means doing the same things repeatedly.

This is exactly where the problem begins. Doing the same thing repeatedly becomes boring for most people, and that's where they slip up. They start off by doing the right activities for some time, but then they get bored and start looking for variety or for different ways of doing things. I am not against experimenting with new ideas, but one should never stop doing the core activities that are essential for success.

Martial arts legend Bruce Lee used to say, *"I fear not the man who has practiced 10,000 kicks once, but I fear the man who has practiced one kick 10,000 times."*

Both success and mastery of any skill require practice and repetition. Identify key activities that you need for success and simply get busy doing them day in and day out. That's the way legends are made.

22

You are not on a mission to create a network marketing-positive world.

When someone complains that people are negative regarding this business, I wonder: if everyone is so negative, how come all stadiums have been full at every network marketing event since the 1940s? India is expecting 1.8 crore Indians to generate sales worth Rs. 64,000 crores in this business by 2025. How can this happen for a business about which people are negative?

Actually, most of these negative people are those who tried and failed at network marketing, and they failed because they did not do the necessary work. Handled well, they will be the first ones to start again. But most of the network marketers who complain about negativity are themselves doubtful about this business. They work half-heartedly with doubts and overreact to every objection.

Even if negativity is there, it's not a problem; it's a feature of the business. When you accept something as a feature, you don't fight with it. You find solutions for it. Fire is hot. That's not a problem but a feature of fire, so you avoid touching it. Accept that people are negative and find ways to handle it.

Anyway, you don't need the whole world to build your business. You just need a few like-minded people who are willing to work with you to fulfill their dreams. Go for them.

23

What brought you here will not take you there.

Your current income, lifestyle, influence, and rank are the result of your current skill level, mindset, and the actions you have taken in the last few months. If you keep doing the same things, you will automatically get the same results. If you want different results, you need to take new actions with a new mindset and skills.

Every dream can be achieved if you are willing to prepare for the same. You cannot earn 5 lakhs per month with the same mindset, skillset, and strategy that you have been using to earn 50,000 per month. In the same way, if you want to build a big passive income-generating business empire, you have to totally elevate your current mindset, beliefs, skills, and working strategy. Your results are the fruits; your mindset, skills, and daily actions are the roots. Work on the roots and the fruits will automatically change.

I have seen lakhs of frustrated network marketers who just write down big dreams, paste pictures everywhere, and continue visualizing them without making any progress. These dreams will never become a reality if they don't improve their mindset, skillset, and working strategy. What brought you here will not take you there.

24

Personal sponsoring is oxygen in network marketing. Your business will die without it.

Everyone starts his or her network marketing business with personal sponsoring. Those who rise to the top 1% of income levels and command great respect in this business continue doing personal sponsoring years after they have started. The fact is that if you cannot do personal sponsoring, you should consider finding some other business for yourself.

What makes an ordinary person earn a big income in this business? Teamwork and duplication. If you don't do personal sponsoring, you cannot build your team, and if you don't do it continuously, your teammates will also follow your example and not do it. So personal sponsoring is one of the key activities to survive and thrive in this business.

If you want to do it but you are lacking the right mindset and skillset, immediately get training from your upline or my online and offline events. Personal sponsoring is not optional; it is essential. It will give you more income, a higher rank, more stability, more confidence, and greater influence.

One more thing: when you started your business, you had no experience and zero achievements. If you could do personal sponsoring back then, then why not now? You know how to do it. Just do it.

25

It's a business, and it will take time.

People are generally willing to work for 3 to 5 years or even more for achieving reasonable success in any business or job. But when it comes to network marketing, people expect 10 times the income and are not willing to devote even 3 to 5 months of committed effort. One of the key reasons behind this mindset is the false expectations with which people venture into this business. Many people consider this business a get-rich-quick scheme or a lottery and when they don't get such results, they start saying this business model does not work.

Anything of lasting value takes time to create. Network marketing is a business like any other, and establishing it with a solid foundation definitely takes time. Building relationships, setting up business centers, establishing tools and systems, and developing leaders take a lot of time and effort. But if you do it the right way and set it up properly on the foundation of education, values, and the right system, it will continue to grow on its own.

Remember, taller buildings need deeper foundations. Patience is an invaluable virtue for every great entrepreneur. Continue the good work and don't rest till you become the best.

26

Big dreams are awesome, but what really matters is how long you can keep those dreams alive.

There has been big hype in network marketing about having big dreams and talking about those big dreams. During big events and company conventions, you will often hear leaders talking about helicopters, private aircrafts, mansions, and islands. That is excellent. Big dreams inspire you to be more and do more. But there is one more thing that is even more important, and that is how long can you keep those dreams alive.

Fulfilling your dreams is the result, and all the work that you need to do to achieve those dreams is what will make them a reality. I have seen people who have certain dreams onstage and entirely different ones offstage. A few prospects say 'no', a few teammates quit, or some family members ridicule them, and all those big dreams instantly disappear.

I believe in two fundamental things about dreams:

- Your dreams should be yours. The main purpose of a dream is to inspire you, not to impress others. They should propel you to action.

- Your dreams should be non-negotiable. You must be willing to do whatever it takes and for however long it takes to make them a reality.

27

If people don't change,
change the people.

The unhappiest and the lowest-income people in this business are the ones who are constantly trying to improve people. They always have complaints about their teammates and keep blaming others for anything bad that happens. They are always on a mission to convert others to their ideology. But the fact remains that people will not change because you want them to change; rather, people will change when change is the only option.

As you start building your team, always remember:

- You should extend the best possible support to everyone who ventures into business with you. Use events and group meetings to support everyone, but give your personal time to those who are committed to do their share of the work.

- Continue doing personal sponsoring every week. It is much easier to get changed people who are ready to work than to change people.

- Whenever you attend or deliver any training or team events, spot people who have the potential to become big business builders and start mentoring them directly.

- Learn more and earn more. As you grow yourself and your achievements, better people will start reaching out to you to join your team.

28

No profession can guarantee respect; respect comes from the ethics and professionalism with which you pursue that profession.

When people tell me that network marketers don't get their due respect in society, I want to say to them, *"Show me one profession in the world where everyone gets equal respect."* There are good doctors, and there are many doctors who bring a bad name to their profession. There are bad lawyers and good ones, too. There are good teachers and many bad ones, too. The same goes for network marketing: there are good network marketers and there are bad ones.

Your profession doesn't guarantee you respect. Respect comes from the ethics and professionalism with which you pursue that profession. Build your business with the right values and you will get more respect than you could imagine.

In many jobs or professions, respect is given not to the person but to their position or designation. When the position goes away, so does the respect. But in network marketing, as you empower people to live their dream lives, they will forever be grateful to you. If you have read my second book on network marketing *Achieve More, Succeed Faster*, you would have read the 31 hidden benefits of network marketing apart from making money. If you help someone get these benefits, how will you not receive an abundance of love and respect?

29

We are not paid for the number of meetings we conduct. We are paid for the sales we generate.

I have seen thousands of people in this business whose results and income have not changed in the last 10 years. There may be temporary ups and downs, but broadly they are at the same income level today that they were at 10 years ago. Interestingly, these people always look busy. They always look tired and their faces are full of stress. Some of them will talk about how they work 14 to 16 hours everyday, and others will talk about how many kilometers they've run on their new car. But these people forget two fundamental laws:

- It's not about the meetings; it's about results. If your car's odometer reading is your benchmark, join the taxi business, not the network marketing business.

- If you keep doing the same things, you will continue getting the same results.

It's not enough to just be busy; get busy doing the right things. It's about productivity and efficiency. You need to analyze your performance either by yourself or with some coach. After the analysis, just do more of what is working and less of what is not working. If some things are not providing results, stop doing them or modify them. Don't prove how hard are you working. Prove your work with your results.

30

Are you growing from event
to event?

This is one question that I have always asked my lakhs of teammates and later my training participants – are you growing from event to event? As a committed leader, every time you attend a network marketing event, check yourself using these two parameters:

- Are you at a better income, rank, or achievement level in this program than where you were in the last program?
- Are more of your teammates attending this event than the last event?

If your answer to these two questions is 'yes', then your business is going in the right direction. But if the number is declining, that's a red flag. Be alert: something has been going wrong in your team. Even if the numbers are the same, that is also a signal that something is going wrong, because it takes a few months for the decline to be visible. So you must quickly spring into massive action on all business basics.

As you grow further, get smarter and track not just the total event numbers but also how many associates have been attending from each different leg. Always remember – event numbers are the lifeblood of the business.

31

Your teammates observe you for months before deciding to commit to the business.

Most of the people who venture into this business never visit the company office or factory before starting. Their meetings never happen with the founder or director of the company but with a friend, neighbor, colleague, or in some cases a stranger whom they have recently come in contact with. Your team would also have started because of you and not your senior leaders or company directors.

Your team ventures into business with you after observing you and your attitude, faith, confidence, commitment, performance, and achievements. These also affect how aggressively they build your business. Everyone in your team carefully observes everything you say or do, both onstage and offstage. I have personally found people who said they watched me for more than a year before deciding to join my team and aggressively build business.

If your leadership qualities are growing, your faith is multiplying, and your achievements are increasing, your teammates will start building the business seriously. But if your performance is not good, they will slowly exit the business. Remember what I said earlier: people don't listen with their ears, they listen with their eyes.

32

I will either find a way or
make a way.

Every single time I have faced a challenge or felt stuck in a situation, I worked with the belief that I will either find a way or make a way. Many times, I couldn't achieve exactly what I had planned, but every single time I worked with this belief, I learned a lot and bettered myself.

Constant change is normal in every business. Situations will not go as per the plan and people will not do as you expect. Old leaders will quit, teams will collapse, new locations will open up, and new leaders will have new demands. As you go through this journey, never forget why you ventured into this business and continue moving forward toward your goals by finding new ways or making new ways.

Trust me, you are much more powerful and resourceful than you think you are. The best of your power will reveal itself when you are under pressure. You will never find out what you have till you are forced to use it. So when life is putting you through challenges, remind yourself that every diamond goes through lot of grinding, and now it's your turn to shine like a diamond.

33

90% of selling is predictable.

One of the biggest fears that stop people from starting a network marketing business is that they will have to do selling. If you also have doubts about your selling ability, just remember these three insights I have realized after training 1.7 million people in sales over the last 2 decades:

- 90% of selling is predictable. Fundamentally, you do two key activities while selling – sharing your business opportunity and handling objections. How to share your opportunity is pre-decided, and you can learn it from your seniors. 90% of the objections that people will raise during the meeting are also known in advance. If you can just prepare and rehearse well, you will be able to answer their concerns like an expert.

- Selling is all about conversation. If you genuinely listen to your prospects' concerns and understand their situation, the meeting will naturally flow toward closing.

- Nobody is born a salesperson; people develop their selling skill like any other skill. When I look at the hard work people do for many years to become doctors, engineers, chartered accountants, etc. I feel like it's relatively faster and easier to master selling. The only challenge is that people are often not committed to learning it.

34

We are looking for people
who are looking.

The number one quality I have always looked for in people before committing to aggressively work with them is their hunger. I have always observed that all top leaders in network marketing across the globe are hungry. They are hungry for growth, leadership, and achievements. They not only write down goals but are also totally committed to do whatever it takes to achieve their goals. Anybody can write their goals in fancy notebooks and forget about them, but those who are really hungry for their goals convert them into daily actions and work untiringly on their daily rituals.

One mistake I have seen a lot of network marketers make is that they judge their new teammates based on their current income, profession, or profile. They consider them high-profile people and focus all their energy on them.

Always remember that this business is simple, but not easy. When anyone starts working in this field, they face a lot of rejection, disappointment, and ridicule. Only those who are hungry for their dreams can withstand these changes and are able to do whatever it takes to achieve their dream lifestyle. So choose your people carefully.

35

People don't come to social media to buy things; people come to interact and connect with people.

If you remember this one rule, most of what you post and do on social media will change forever. Social media is not a place for shopping; social media is a platform to connect and interact with people. Yes, your objective is to sell more products and get new teammates, but you cannot achieve this by posting constantly about your products or business. What will people do if the only thing they see on your page all the time is related to your product or opportunity? They will unfollow or block you.

Always remember that posts are different from advertisements and that your page is definitely not a billboard. As a general rule, don't post about your company, products, income proofs, Zoom links, meeting invitations, etc. on your page.

If you want to learn the right way to build a big business online using social media, learn from an expert or explore my online course, Social Media & Online Business Mastery. Never forget that your social media page is a place to showcase who you are and what you are passionate about. Your page will make people like you and connect with you. You can later approach them for business separately using a sales funnel.

36

Success loves speed.

Success happens in stages. If you build your business quickly and achieve your first few goals faster, it creates momentum that helps you achieve bigger goals easier and faster. This series of achievements will gradually establish your brand as a fast achiever.

In 2007, when I started my network marketing career, I resigned from my job within 3 months, broke many records in my company, and purchased my first Mercedes Benz within 2 years. Those records established my brand as a record-breaking machine and propelled me to accomplish even bigger achievements faster.

People venture into the network marketing business to fulfill their dreams faster, and big achievements are not possible without speed. All your teammates will stay with you and follow you if you are a leader with rapid achievements. Even new prospects like to join someone who has notable achievements.

So if you are committed to fulfilling your dreams through this business, increase your speed. One sure fireway to increase your speed is to show the next month's plans this month itself. 100 plans shown in one month have totally different results and impact compared to 100 plans shown in one year. Work with speed and make speed a part of your team's culture.

37

Remember the KLT rule of selling: people love to do business with those they know, like, and trust.

Why do I recommend you venture into this business by approaching people you already know? Why do I recommend you build rapport and credibility before sharing your business plan? Why does it take more time and effort to convert strangers to teammates than your friends or acquaintances? Why is it important to use social media in the right way to set up your prospecting pool and follow-through pool? The answer lies in the KLT rule.

All of us prefer to buy things from some particular shops or brands even when the same item is available at the same price at many different places. When everything else is the same, we always prefer to buy from or do business with those whom we know, like, and trust. That is the KLT rule of selling.

Every time you are prospecting, meeting people online or offline, or posting anything on social media, ask yourself – will whatever you are doing enable your prospects to know you, like you, or trust you more? If you can align all your actions with the KLT rule, it will totally change your game and put your business on the fast track to success.

38

Working with the right people is
an investment. Working with the
wrong people is an expense.

Network marketing is a business of leadership, and your key task is to constantly create leaders in your team. There are four core activities for creating more leaders in your team:

- Developing your own leadership qualities and accomplishing big achievements quickly.
- Providing complete new age training to your teammates to build their faith, confidence, skills, mindset, and capabilities.
- Working with your associates in the field.
- Getting personal counseling for yourself from a coach and providing counseling to your team.

All these activities need a lot of time, and time never comes back once gone. If you invest this time with the right people, they will develop accountability, competency, and leadership. They will start working independently and build more leaders within the team. But when you give your time to people who are not committed, all your time is wasted.

Hence it is extremely important to select the right people to work with. Also, as you grow in this business, you will be traveling the world and celebrating your success with your key leaders. If they are the right people, you will not only be rich but also happy. Your time is your biggest resource. Choose wisely before you give it to anyone.

39

You have not really sponsored a person until you make them sponsor someone else.

Do you know some network marketers who have built a team of 50, 100, or even 500 but whose income remains the same, and who continue struggling year after year? Actually, most network marketers believe that getting a sale is the last step in our business. This is the biggest mistake you can make, because getting a sale is not the end but the beginning of the business.

Most people conduct meetings after meetings and calls after calls and do everything possible to close one sale, but once the person ventures into the business, they either stop all those activities or just put in 10% of the effort they did to get the sale.

The top income earners in network marketing focus on the right take-off for their associates. They create a system so that everyone who joins their team gets the right take-off when venturing into the business. As a rule of thumb, always remember that you get a new person on your team only after they have done their first sale.

If your income is not multiplying even though a lot of new people are coming into your team, it's high time to review the take-off system for your team.

40

When you have been labeled as someone who is in the business of recruiting people, why don't you aggressively recruit more people?

A countless number of talented people with big dreams and capabilities are never able to take off in this business because they keep doing everything other than personal sponsoring. You will find many leaders who have stopped personal sponsoring under the excuse that they have been busy supporting their team.

Whatever your excuse is, please remember that getting new associates or customers in this business is not an option; it's an essential requirement. Performing surgeries and treating people is a doctor's daily job. A lawyer presents arguments for their clients and an architect creates new building designs everyday. Likewise, a network marketer survives and thrives only when he or she gets new people into the business and empowers them to build the business further. If you think you cannot do personal sponsoring, please don't waste any more time and leave this business right now.

The moment you venture into this business, the whole world puts a label on you, saying that you are in the business of recruiting people. When everyone around you thinks that you are recruiting people into your business, why don't you do it, and do it aggressively?

41

If you are not able to achieve your goal, change your strategy or actions, but never the goal.

Everytime you start taking new actions to achieve a goal, you will inevitably meet with challenges and setbacks. People and situations will surprise you and the results will be different from what you expected. That is the defining moment in every career, where the winners are separated from the losers and the diamonds are separated from the coal.

What you need to observe when you face failure or disappointment is your internal dialogue, i.e. everything you say to yourself. When a tough situation occurs, most people get into a trap I call EBC disease – they Excuse, Blame or Complain. But in the same situation, winners get creative and look for alternate solutions.

I have realized that problems are inevitable milestones on your way to success. Failure is feedback. If your actions didn't yield the desired results, it's not time to quit; it's time to try something else. It's not the time to whine. It's time to be creative. In fact, this is the only way to grow.

We don't grow when everything is going great; we grow only when plans fail. Remember that real work starts when the plan falls apart. Just ask yourself – *what is the best thing you can do right now? And get moving.*

42

Communication and momentum
are a network marketer's
best friends.

Every business has some core activities that directly lead to results and productivity. In network marketing, there is no office, no boss, and no formal authority. So what keeps this business going? Communication. You can use virtual one-on-one meetings, phone calls, WhatsApp messages, and other online communication tools, but the best form of communication is having a face-to-face meeting. In all network marketing teams – small or big, new or old, located in a metro city or a small village – meetings are the lifeblood of the business and keep it running.

People get a shared vision, confidence, faith, and team spirit by attending meetings and events. People who don't attend meetings are generally the first ones to quit. Meetings are the place where people get to know of each other's achievements and where one person's speed and achievements get converted into team momentum. Teams that have momentum accomplish achievements that are 3 to 5 times bigger, and they do it faster. Momentum is not possible without meetings.

Remember this rule–the more meetings your team has, the bigger your income and more stable your business. So stay connected to your team through business presentations, strategy meetings, hall meetings, product demonstrations, and specialized network marketing events.

43

God gives you only as much
challenge as you are capable of
handling.

Imagine you reach home with two full shopping bags– one big and one small. Your two sons, aged 10 and 7, come running to you. Whom will you give the heavier bag to? Every time I ask this question to an audience, I get a reply from someone saying they'd give the heavier bag to the 10-year-old and the lighter one to the 7-year-old. Why? Being a parent, you know what kind of load each of your children can handle, and you will give them only as much of a challenge as they can easily handle.

We all are children of God. If we know what load to give to each of our children, God definitely knows better, so He will give you only as much of a challenge as you can easily handle.

During those times when every door seems to be closing on you and all you feel is hopelessness, please remember you already have the strength to overcome whatever challenges you are going through. You are ready. You are capable. You have everything it takes. Take a leap of faith and move forward.

44

"One day I will be successful in this business." That's a prayer, not a business strategy.

When most network marketing leaders or trainers share their story onstage, they end it with a typical line – "If I can do it, then you can, too." Most network marketing programs are full of recognition and motivational stories and declarations in the name of training. People come back from these programs with the fake illusion that one day, they will also be successful, but this fake motivation fades away after a day or so and people quit in frustration.

If you cannot find a job that pays Rs. 50,000 a month without studying for at least 3 to 5 years and investing lakhs of rupees, then how can you expect to be successful in this business without investing time and money into transforming yourself into a successful network marketer?

If you want to become the best, learn from the best. The world is changing fast, and today's business cannot be done with the training, skills and techniques, of the past. Learn from your upline and company training system and complement it with special training from genuine industry experts. If your son fails a class, you change the teacher – you don't stop his education. If you are not getting the results you expect, don't change the business, change your training and working systems. The more you learn, the more you earn.

45

$$I = N^2$$

Income/Influence = Number of active distributors.

This one formula can be your breakthrough in the network marketing business, and I strongly believe this should be your ultimate goal. If you want a big income in this business, never think about your income, just work on increasing the number of active distributors in your team. If the number of active distributors in your team is increasing, your income and influence will automatically increase. So make a leg-wise list of active distributors in your team every month and focus on increasing this number month after month.

Some of you may be great at retailing products. That's fantastic, but never forget that your business will multiply when you convert these customers into distributors or active business builders. Products don't move people; people move products. You can define for yourself whom you consider an active distributor and then track the number of active distributors. I have also provided an Active Distributor Score Card with the 15 essential attributes in my first book, *Be a Network Marketing Millionaire.*

Remember, you are only as big as your team, and you are only as powerful as your team. So grow yourself and continue cultivating leaders in your team.

46

Fortune lies in follow through.

I can sum up my 2 decades of sales experience with this one line – fortune lies in follow through. Every one of your prospects will join you someday if you have the commitment and maturity to continue the follow-through process. You are in this business because you have faith in it. When you are able to transfer this faith to your prospect, the sale is closed. Sometimes it takes 2 meetings and sometimes it may take 5 or 10 to transfer that faith, so your goal should be to continue with the follow-through process till the sale is closed.

The tragedy is most network marketers either don't conduct follow-through meetings or conduct them only to ask the prospect whether they're ready to start or not. Actually, follow-through meetings are where the prospect will ask questions and discuss their past experiences. This is where you get the opportunity to build their faith and confidence. I always told my teammates that you should never share a business opportunity if you cannot commit to 3 to 5 follow-through meetings in next one month.

Put all the sales that you could not close this month in your follow-through pool and continue the process professionally and without annoying the prospect.

47

The genius lies not in getting people,
but in retaining people.

Most people feel that it's tough to get people into the network marketing business, but it is even tougher to retain people and to convert them into active business builders. Your business will scale up and you will earn big passive income only when those who start with you stay and actively work with you. Try these four team retention strategies that have worked for thousands of my trainees:

- Make your new associates use your company products. Give them all the product information and testimonies. If they are happy with the products, they will regularly repurchase them and confidently recommend them to others.

- Give your team the best environment that inspires them to stay in the business. If you are able to build a culture of values, ethics, family bonding, relationships, and edification, people will love to stay with your team.

- Develop the right take-off system for new associates. If new associates develop the right foundation, their chances of staying in the business multiply.

- Teach them something that adds value to their lives and helps them become better people. Give them holistic, all-round development training that is truly transformative.

48

An army of sheep led by a lion will
always beat an army of lions
lead by a sheep.

This business is all about leadership.

No leadership = No network marketing

Great leadership = Great business empire

When you start in this business, you are part of some leader's team. Everyone starts like this, but as you grow your business, you need to develop your leadership abilities and emerge as a great leader. Only a great leader can attract and create more leaders. When you are a great leader, good prospects will come to your team. Your teammates will feel confident working in your team. Team retention and performance will multiply and people will follow your strategies.

Leadership in network marketing begins with your achievements in the business. Stop making excuses."I am busy supporting the team", "I am only focusing on one leg right now", "I am a part-timer", "I don't have experience", "People are negative", "My list is over", "I am new" – these excuses will destroy your business.

Developing your leadership skills is your top responsibility. Become an achiever. Learn more, attend special training programs, work everyday, upgrade your skills, develop your mindset, work with a coach, win contests, arrange special training programs for your team, focus on your own leadership development, and build your business with absolute commitment.

49

You can have only one of these in
your pocket – ego or success.
It's your choice.

Countless numbers of smart, talented, and already successful people are unable to build their network marketing business because of two simple reasons:

- They try to build their network marketing business in the same way they built their existing career. They forget that there are different personality traits, skills, and strategies for success in different businesses, jobs, and professions. What brought you massive success as a doctor cannot make you a successful entrepreneur or CEO. Likewise, if you want to become a successful direct seller, you need to become a student of direct selling and work with the principles and strategies of this business.

- Initial success sometimes breeds the illusion in people that they know everything. Please remember that you came to this business for growth. Your current set of knowledge and skills has already given you all the success that it can. If you want to grow further, you need to learn new things and upgrade yourself.

Learn this business and work with the right system and strategies. Remember, the goal is not to show off your past success or knowledge; the goal is to become successful in this new business.

50

Never confuse intimation with
invitation. Those who master new
age invitation skills will always have
a stable and progressive business.

Getting people to venture into this business is not difficult. The real challenge is to convert them into serious business builders, and that happens when you shift their belief, confidence, and attitude toward the business. This shift happens only during events. Hence inviting people to events is a critical skill for success in this business.

For most people, an invitation means forwarding a Zoom link to a WhatsApp group or posting event invitations on their social media accounts. This is not an invitation, it's only an intimation, and nobody comes to an event solely on an intimation.

So if you are committed to building your business, put more life and effort into inviting your teammates to events. You need to conduct multiple calls, meetings, and reminder calls to get people to come to events. When you ask someone to join your event for 2 hours, there will be many other people or events that are seeking those same 2 hours from that person. So as a rule of thumb, your invitation should be so strong that your invitees make it a priority to attend your event and leave aside all other engagements.

Invitation is an undervalued skill in network marketing training. Focus on it and master it quickly.

51

The spark in your eyes and glow on your face will close more sales than all the product knowledge or presentation skills you have.

Your product knowledge and business plan are definitely important, but they're not enough to close a sale. If that was the case, companies would just email excellent business presentation videos to lakhs of people and sales would start pouring in.

Please remember, people don't venture into the network marketing business just to buy another soap, health supplement, or fairness cream; people do so for the opportunity to fulfill their dreams and transform their lives. People choose you because they hope that your association and guidance will help them succeed faster.

Most of your prospects will have already seen similar products and presentations, but you are what is unique. Your words may lie, but not your body language and subconscious mind. Hence the spark in your eyes, the confidence in your words, the glow on your face, and excitement of working toward your dreams serve as your biggest sales closers.

The spark and glow show when you are truthful, well-prepared, have absolute faith in your company and products, know your products and business in and out, and have full conviction in the business. Build your business on the foundation of ethics and professionalism, and success will definitely be yours.

52

Be a master of edification and uplift
people at every opportunity.

Network marketing is a people business, and uplifting people is part of the job description. Use every interaction with people to uplift them. Remember the golden rule – leave people better than you found them.

Trust and respect does not come with your ID; you need to earn them. One of the best ways to earn respect is to give it. Respect people regardless of their age, background, profession, rank, or financial situation. Stand with your people. Be with them in their good and bad times.

Real security never comes from money; security comes from relationships. As per Hindu mythology, Lord Ram was exiled for 14 years just one day before his coronation. His palace and all his riches disappeared overnight, but his brother and wife stayed with him. The same idea is also mentioned in the Mahabharata. Everything was taken away from the Pandavas, but the brothers stayed together through everything and rose again.

Leaving aside business, even just being a human being, you ought to encourage and support your fellow human beings. Everyone is going through their own challenges, and your words can encourage them to move forward. It doesn't cost any money, so why not do it with all your heart?

53

Show me your calendar, and
I will predict the size of your
achievements and the quality of
your life.

Life is measured in days. If your days are going well, your life is going well. If you manage your days well, your life will automatically be well-managed. Network marketers are excellent at setting 5 to 10 year goals, but when it comes to planning their days, most of them just leave it to chance or willpower.

Please understand that if you plan and focus on your 5-year goals, you may not achieve them, but if you carefully plan and execute your days, you will definitely achieve them. It's so important that during my live event, UCY (Unleash the Champion in You), we invest 5 hours on scheduling your day through a unique process using a 100-page workbook.

You need to become selfish about your time and start valuing it more. Keep a close watch on who and what you give your time to everyday. Work with a calendar. If better health is part of your 5-year plan, you must devote some part of your day to your health. If your family is your priority, it must be on your calendar. Whatever is important to you must be on your calendar. Your calendar doesn't lie.

54

The fastest way to reach the top rank of your company is to quickly convert individuals to teams.

Who ventures into business with you? Individuals. Who goes to the top? Individuals who become leaders and build their own teams. Individuals start the business; teams reach the top. The most successful people in this business are those who know the art of converting individuals to teams quickly.

Network marketers struggle for years without any success because most of them have been trained to approach the business like fishing, where you cast out a net and keep waiting for some fish to get caught in your net through the Law of Attraction, affirmations, positive thinking, and motivation. If something is important for the business, you cannot leave it to chance.

You need to build systems for every important business activity:

- What are the different events associates should attend every month?
- What are the different tools that will be shared with associates at different stages of building business?
- What are your criteria for identifying future leaders?
- What are the specialized programs you offer for different levels of leaders?
- How will you train the trainers or presenters to host events, product demonstrations, basic training, business opportunity presentations or business plan presentations, leadership training, business skill training, etc.?

55

It's not about part-time or full-time. It's about doing the right activities with the right people at the right time.

You will hear many network marketers say that they are not able to build a big business only because they are doing it part-time along with their job, profession, or some other business. This is totally false and just a lame excuse to cover their non-performance.

No direct selling company gives different commissions to part-timers and full-timers. We are paid on volume generated in the right structure. Ambanis and Tatas are running hundreds of businesses. Which business is part-time and which one is full-time? If they can run so many businesses simultaneously, why can't you manage your job or profession along with your network marketing business?

Please remember – it's not about part-time or full-time, it's about focusing on the business basics every day and building the right team. You need to focus on the business and commit consistent time to building it every day. If you can't focus on the business properly working part-time, you will never be able to do it properly full-time. But at the same time, if your income is stable and your business is expanding rapidly, you must switch to becoming a full-timer. Not giving your time to your business in that situation can badly affect your growth.

56

If you are not happy while building your business, you are doing something wrong.

Raise your ambitions and set big goals. Hustle more today than yesterday. Dream of big cars, mansions, private jets, and every luxury possible. All these things are great. The problem starts when you attach your happiness to your achievements. Never forget that your work and constant improvement are entirely your responsibility, but the results may not always be in your control.

So if you say you will only be happy when you have that car or house or rank, you have chosen months or years of daily misery as you work toward your goal. Keep your eyes on the goal, but enjoy the process. My son Saksham says that the game most rewards the player for whom the game itself is the biggest reward. Fall in love with the process. Make happiness your life compass. If you are not happy with Rs.10,000 in income, you will not be happy even when your income goes to 10 lakhs.

Also, don't confuse happiness with satisfaction. I may not be satisfied with my current position, but I can still be happy. Happiness is a decision; just choose to be happy and continue working toward your goals. If you work happily, success will also come faster.

57

Make more mistakes and fail
more often.

If you ever meet someone who has never made a mistake, be rest assured they are someone who has never tried anything new. Whenever you do anything new, you will make mistakes. Mistakes and failures are your medals. Mistakes are proof that you are trying. If you learn from your mistake, it is no longer a mistake – it's an invaluable experience that can totally change your future. At the same time, please remember that if you keep repeating the same mistake, it is no longer a mistake – it's a decision.

My son Saksham is a pro basketball player, and he always tells me that the real game is not physical but emotional. How do you build your emotional muscles? By acting in spite of fear and setbacks. Let fear do its work and you do yours. Fear will only haunt you till you face it.

Teams may crash and people may leave, but you can always bounce back. That is how you become a real leader. Don't stop till you become a leader you are proud of. You have everything it takes. This is your time. Now is your turn. Make it happen. The industry needs you.

58

Stability and growth are automatic if you build your business on the foundation of ethics and the right education.

If you want stability and constant growth in your business, then make ethics and the right education the foundation of your business. If training programs are merely motivational seminars and the focus is to squeeze maximum sales from a customer one way or another, you are playing the short-term game.

If you treat this business like a scheme or lottery, this business will reward you correspondingly, but if you build this business with the right ethics, values, training, and systems, this business will continue to yield wealth, recognition, and joy generation after generation.

Here are a few fundamental rules that you and your team must follow everyday:

- Never tell a lie.
- Never commit to something that you cannot honor later.
- Treat others' family members with the utmost respect and maintain appropriate behavior.
- If someone gives you money for products or tickets; deliver the same to them in time.
- Never speak negatively to anyone, not even your downlines or crosslines.
- There should be no loans between upline and downline.
- Treat everyone with respect regardless of their age, profession, education, financial background, language, or location.
- Never put any job or profession down to show that your opportunity is better.

59

Don't change your track because of those who are not on track themselves.

When you start discussing this business opportunity with people, you will hear stories about failures and negativity in this business. If you give 3 reasons why people should venture into business with you; they will immediately give you 30 reasons why you should also quit.

Most network marketers don't realize that when people say nobody succeeds in this business, it's just their opinion and not a fact. When someone says this business doesn't work, they just want to convey that they have tried venturing into this business in the past but did not succeed. If you probe deeper, you will find that in the majority of these cases, they did not do the basics, their upline quit, or they chose the wrong company. People try to hide their failure by blaming it on the business.

I want to remind you that if you want to enjoy what only the top 1% of people have, then do what top 1% of people do. Never ask for an advice about buying a BMW from someone who is hunting for the cheapest second hand car. In any game, players don't make the noise; it's the audience who makes the noise. The players just focus on the game and make money.

60

Stop complaining about your upline; start working to become a great upline yourself.

As you start growing your business, conflicts will rise between the upline and downline. These are natural, and most genuine ones can be resolved with open conversation, but if the conflicts are due to ego, insecurity, forced leadership, or wrong intentions, you need to take a stand and do what is right.

Every leader has made it big by taking full ownership of their business. It's your business, and when you decide to learn more, do more, and be more, every upline should be happy. But if someone is uncomfortable with your growth, please don't stop growing. You have not started your business to please your upline or downline; you started your business to fulfill your dreams and live life on your terms.

Stay focused and work everyday on becoming a great upline. It may be tough and require lot of hard work, but if you are able to accomplish this, you will be a leader for life. Start with what you have and from where you are. If you are willing to learn, you will find the right mentor, training, and support to help you become your best version. Go for it and claim your place.

From My Heart to Yours

Congratulations on choosing this incredible business opportunity to fulfill your dreams. Since 2007, I have trained more than 1.7 million network marketers and I must tell you that now is the best time in the history of the world to join this business. The 60 key insights and strategies in this book can totally change your life and business if you implement them diligently. My team and I are always there to support you on your journey to achieving your dreams. On top of these 60 insights, I want to share with you a few parting thoughts that are close to my heart.

Wherever you reach and whatever you achieve, never stop learning and growing. My coach always tells me that the question is not where you reached here from, the question is where you can go from here. Make constant improvement your life philosophy, because every next level of success demands the next version of you. If you are willing to learn, nothing can stop you, but if you are not ready to learn, nobody can help you. Invest in yourself. To become the best, learn from the best. The amount spent on training is not an expense, but an investment for your future.

As you continue growing as an upline, give wings to your team. Let them fly. Let them rise. Support them, but don't overshadow them, and don't come in the way of their growth. Don't force respect or leadership. Earn it. If you believe that you and your system are perfect, let them go anywhere. The right people will come back to you.

Don't work to impress people, work to grow yourself and be a totally different person today than you were a year ago. Don't be in a hurry to build houses or a collection of cars; build people. First you build people, then the people will build the business.

Everyone talks about what they have got out of this industry – cars, houses, foreign trips, income, etc. What this industry needs today are people who think about what they can give to the industry. I invite you to start thinking about ways in which you can contribute to the industry. Together, let's bring more pride and glory to this beautiful profession.

For the last few years, I have been building a community of network marketers who are willing to contribute to the industry – a community of like-minded people who are committed to rise, evolve, and then give back to the industry. If you are interested, message me on any of my social media accounts or email me and we will tell you more about our mission.

Never forget: the magic lies in implementation and action. Share and apply everything you have learned from this book.

I have one dream – I want to see you at the top.

Learn more. Do more. Be more.

I am already proud of you.

Love and strength,
—Deepak

Deepak Bajaj's Solutions for Life and Business Transformation

Every next level of success demands a different version of you.

For almost two decades, I have been passionately obsessed with creating tools and trainings to empower people to accomplish their dreams easier and faster. All my books, training, videos, online courses, workshops, speeches, and everything else that I do are centered on this mission. I strongly believe all of us have the seeds of greatness within us and can accomplish amazing achievements with the right inspiration, training, and mentoring. My team and I want to contribute in your journey to success, happiness, and abundance through our research-based, practical, proven, and constantly evolving tools and solutions.

All my tools and trainings have been designed with one clear goal in mind –they should bring instant change and lasting transformation. I also believe that success is empty without peace, health, relationships, and fulfilment. So everything we do has been designed to provide you holistic and sustainable transformation. Although people call me a motivational speaker, I believe that motivation is temporary; only transformation is permanent. Team Deepak Bajaj has got a wide range of resources available for total life and business transformation. You can find all the updated details on our website (www.deepakbajaj.biz) and our social media accounts. Here is a glimpse of our major tools and solutions:

There is no secret to success; there is always a system to success.

– Deepak Bajaj

#1. Free Video Training: Deepak's YouTube Channel is considered one of the most trusted, transformative, and biggest free training resources available online. You will find a huge collection of life-changing training videos full of the knowledge, tools, ideas, and techniques to take your life and business to the next level. You will find 550+ videos on direct selling/network marketing, relationships, teambuilding, success, goals, social media mastery, leadership, time management, life management, public speaking, communication, and a lot of other subjects at www.youtube.com/deepakbajaj. As of my writing of this book in October 2022, this channel has a community of 8.7 lakh subscribers and 40 million views from 150+ countries.

#2. Online Courses: You can master the best international knowledge, tools, skills, and ideas right from your mobile phone with Deepak's cutting-edge online courses. These courses have been designed and delivered with a unique NLP-based methodology, activity-based learning, tasks, and community support so that you get incredible results even though you are doing them online.

#3. Books: What you are holding in your hand is the fourth book by Deepak Bajaj. Deepak's other 3 books *Be a Social Media Millionaire, Achieve More, Succeed Faster,* and *Be a*

Network Marketing Millionaire have been among the most-read and most-followed books in the direct selling industry. These are essential guidebooks that have already given excellent results to lakhs of direct sellers across the globe irrespective of their company, products, or income plan. You can order them online from all major e-retailers or get them from any bookstore near you. Deepak has written some excellent e-books as well that you can download totally free of cost from our website (www.deepakbajaj.biz).

#4. Live Training Events: Deepak's live training events are your best opportunity to learn live from him and experience the transformation for yourself. His events are famous for their incredible energy and real-life transformations that begin right during the event. As of the writing of this book, more than 1.7million people have already attended these workshops and training events. These workshops are always packed with a full house due to their unique methodology, result-delivering activities, best international course material, transformative tools, and real-life techniques.

#5. High-Performance Coaching: For those who want to achieve nothing but the best at jet speed, there is a high-performance coaching program where Deepak personally works with you to create customized solutions to take you or your organization to the next level of excellence in whatever area you choose – health, happiness, profitability, business multiplication, emotional challenges, etc.

#6. Keynote Speeches: Deepak has been regularly invited by corporates, universities, direct selling companies, and various independent bodies to deliver his unique, electrifying, and transformative speeches that not only motivate the audience but also produce the desired results. Deepak provides unique tools and techniques during the speeches that add high value to distributor meets, annual functions, leadership training programs, and company conventions. These speeches generally run from 30 minutes to 2 hours long and are customized as per the needs of the organizers. Deepak works with a unique 6-component formula to deliver transformation with every speech.

#7. Customized Training: Deepak and his team conduct customized training on variety of subjects for corporates, universities, direct selling companies, and direct selling teams. Deepak's corporate experience, international NLP certification, and 19 years of experience training more than 1.7 million people bring instant change and lasting transformation with every training session that he conducts. Deepak is the number one choice for training for all major network marketing companies.

Get all the necessary information at:

www.deepakbajaj.biz

The end of one journey is the beginning of another one.

–Deepak Bajaj

Looking forward to meeting you again soon.

Gratitude

My sincere gratitude to each and every one of my readers, social media followers, workshop and event participants, coaching clients, teammates, and every one of you who have touched my life with your presence and wisdom. Every interaction with you has deeply impacted me and made me the person I am today. I can never thank you enough for all your ever-growing love, support, and prayers. This book is all yours. Thanks a lot.

I have an incredible 24/7 support system who is behind everything I do – my family. I am lucky to have found all of these in my family – my best friends, companions, partners, advisors, cheerleaders, and my biggest supporters. I am nothing without all the love, care, support, affection, and inspiration you all give me. Thank you Papa, Mamma, Tanima, Gaurav, Divya, Devanshi, Cheeraayu, Prashansa, Nirbhay,and Saksham.

Special thanks to my brother and partner Gaurav Bajaj. He is the backbone behind all our achievements and the best network marketing leader I have ever seen in my life.

www.ingramcontent.com/pod-product-compliance
Lightning Source LLC
Chambersburg PA
CBHW031943190326
41519CB00007B/636